Insights 3
A Journey Beyond Boundaries

By Dr. Jaya Sonkar, MD MPH

Photograph by: Dr. Jaya Sonkar MD MPH

HOBBIES AND HAPPINESS CREATIONS
Texas, USA

Published by Hobbies and Happiness Creations 2024
Copyright Dr. Jaya Sonkar MD MPH 2024

Dedication

This book is dedicated to my daughter, Ms. Riya Agarwal; my beloved parents, Mr. Ram Baboo Sonkar and Mrs. Ranjana Sonkar; and my cherished family and friends. I extend my heartfelt gratitude to my teachers, patients, colleagues, business partners, vendors, and everyone I have ever met. Each meeting and every interaction has contributed to my learning journey, and the process continues.

Preface

It has been a journey, a long one, and there is still a long way to go.

Just when I feel I have learned a great deal, something happens to remind me that I have only touched the edges of a small pond, while an ocean of lessons still waits to be discovered.

Medicine is one of the noblest professions. It brings us close to countless lives and gives us the privilege of helping others. Along the way, it offers moments of realization, experiences to grow from, and lessons that shape who we are.

Whether it is the happiest, most content patient or one who is deeply distressed, each carries a unique story filled with wisdom.

Exploring and learning may not have been the goal at the beginning, but they become the very essence of the journey. From beginning to end, life is full of possibilities and opportunities, chances to make choices, to learn from them, and to gather pearls of wisdom along the way.

And perhaps the end is not an end at all, but the beginning of a journey beyond boundaries!

A Note to My Readers

Life is short, even if it lasts a hundred years. Along the way, we will experience everything: joy and sorrow, success and failure, love and even betrayal. We should just expect it, let it come, and then let it pass. Watch it all as if we are spectators, and take the lessons life offers. We should neither let excitement nor despair affect us.

Not long ago, a kind and noble teacher who works with children with special needs shared her struggles. She was trying to stay calm in the middle of her challenges.

The truth is simple: We should do what we can. And what we cannot do, we shouldn't punish ourself for it.

We are human. If we were meant to be perfect, we would not be here. We are not gods. We are here to learn, to stumble, and to grow.

As long as our intentions are good and we give it our best effort, there is nothing to regret. Only lessons to carry forward.

We should try to rest in the middle place between excitement and fear, between joy and sorrow. That balance is where peace lives. And in that stillness, the soul finds room to grow and to thrive.

Index

Contents

Poems

1. WE ARE SUFFICIENT

We are all good, we are all bad, we are all nothing, we are all everything! We are sufficient!

Not everyone is the same
Not everyone likes the same things
Not everyone can do the same things
Not everyone can get along with everyone or anyone But everyone is important
Everyone is needed
And everyone is sufficient

There are supposedly 5 main elements:
- Fire
- Air
- Space
- Earth
- Water

Are these the same?
No.

Do we need all ?
Yes

Do they complement each other?
Yes

In different combinations can they make unique creations?
Yes

Are there different types of works or tasks in the world to sustain it?
Yes

Can one person do it all?
No

Would different people need different qualities to accomplish different things?
Yes

Is it important to have different types of people to do different things?
Yes

Let's take a pause and think about the above questions and answers...

We need variations and differences to be able to survive together as a community.

When no two people can be the same and when we need different people, we should be able to accept their differences.

An adventurous person cannot be homely but can do wonders for the whole world.

A homely person can provide passionate and care and be nurturing.

An experimental person can try different things and bring more options for everyone by discovering new things.

A committed person can commit to things and take them to excellence.

We all think we are the best.
Aren't we our favorites?

We always seem to be right in our eyes. It always seems like the other person is at fault.

Can we say that everyone has something good and everyone has something bad?

Can we say that we are all capable of doing good things and bad things?

Can we say that circumstances and surroundings have a role to play in the events around us?

Can we say we can modify the circumstances and events around us to make things good or bad to a certain extent?
Yes?

Then, we have the power to extract good or bad from the other to a certain extent?

Can we make others do what we want?
No

Can we make us do what we want?
Yes

Then who should we reach out to modify the surroundings to get a desired outcome?

To ourselves.

And that's why we should always ask ourselves what could we have done differently to have had a more favorable outcome and would doing so have been a right thing or wrong?

If it seems right and doesn't harm anyone, then we should do it to modify the surroundings and bring out the goodness in ourselves as well as in others. Fire can never calm a fire down.

If you need to calm a fire then air, space and earth may not be as beneficial but water can do wonders here.

If we need to use the fire to heat up a place, then water may not be the best element. Perhaps some air can blow it up further.

If we use the right element to get the right desired effect, we can do wonders.

Some people are born with an inherent talent to use the right element for the desired effects. Some will have to develop it.

However, it only helps if done with good intentions and get good results that may be of benefit to one and all.

If done with a wrong desire or intention, then it does good to no one.

We all feel like we are good and we are right but we have to know that this is what everyone feels.

Hence, we should all feel the best in our lives but understand that the others are best in their lives.

We are all good, we are all bad, we are all nothing, we are all everything!

But the most important is that we are all sufficient! We are all sufficient together!

Without each other, we won't exist.
We can all do our own things peacefully and survive collectively!

We are all good, we are all bad! We are all positives, we are all negatives. Because the net result of all forces has to be a zero to have an equilibrium!

Photograph by: Dr. Jaya Sonkar MD MPH

2. STRENGTH IS WITHIN

Strength is within
Validation is within
Peace is within
Joy is within
Distractions are outside.

Observing the distractions and taking the learnings from them and absorbing them within to grow, makes distractions a learning experience. Then, growth comes from within.

The societal norm to be with someone is beneficial to protect children. If we bring a life in this world, then protecting and nurturing it, is our first responsibility.

Other than that, self growth and evolution is the main purpose why we are here. And the life should only be shared with someone who facilitates this growth. Any company that pulls it back is not worth keeping.

Doesn't waking up in the morning and making oneself a cup of tea and sitting in the garden observing nature while introspecting and learning more about life in general, sound relaxing and peaceful.

Oftentimes, spending time alone amidst nature (nature can be the grass and sky in our backyard) is very nurturing and motivating.

As part of my work, I often come across brilliant and vibrant patients, some are young and some are elderly. They all have rich experiences to share.

The tougher anyone's journey has been, the more spiritually evolved that individual seems to be.

It is said that the more someone learns, the more they realize that there is a lot more to learn. The more knowledgeable a person is, the kinder that person becomes

As part of providing care to the senior patients, I get fortunate to get a wealth of knowledge and wisdom just by spending some time with them. In the senior population, I find both elderly women and men.

It is known that women outlive males. I see more elderly women than men in very advanced ages. More often than not, they are very mature spiritually at that phase of life.

They enjoy their lives just as much and they are more focused on themselves and their surroundings.

They realize that anything that is there, will pass, be it good or bad.

It's like classes in a school, some people enjoy Math's and Science , some people enjoy language and some geography , some history and some economics.

Not everyone enjoys every subject.

But everyone should learn at least the basics of everything to be able to successfully pass.

Lessons sink deep in the mind when we can concentrate and sit with ourselves and pay full attention to learning the lesson at hand. We can do group studies but end of the day, it's when we sit alone with that book that the deep understanding of the subject comes.

At the end, everyone experiences some time alone.

Be it at the death or be it at the end of life or be it at any phase of life.

And it is at that time that a deep realization comes.

A realization that until that realization came, we didn't really give enough time to ourselves to know ourselves and our own potential.

How many times do we find doing things out of duty, and while ignoring our deep wishes. And how joyful it is to be able to live freely and unrestricted.

Once one experiences this, there is no going back.

We don't need to become famous or millionaires to become truly rich within.

Richness is that of spirit and wealth is that of inner peace.

One can continue to offer love, kindness, help and protection in a detached way.

Why detached?
Detached, so the wealth of joy and peace within is not dependant on anything from outside.

This doesn't mean that one has to seclude oneself. One can be among the crowd sharing bonds of humanity and offering kind hand to others. And yet be in full control of oneself.

After all, we owe some time and attention to this mind and body in which we live.

Because,
Strength is within
Energy is within
Joy is within
Peace is within
Harmony is within
Knowledge is within
Wisdom is within
And
Happiness is within

Drive your own life and set your soul free!

Photograph by: Dr. Jaya Sonkar MD MPH

3. CAN WE DO IT ALL?

Can we do it all?

If one is the only person on the earth, can one do it all?

Water
Electricity
Food
Clothing
Construction
Transport
Safety
Mining
Many more...

May be one can,

Would that be comfortable and to the same level of standards as we have today?
Probably No.

That means we need more people.
That means we need different personalities.
That means we need different tendencies.
That means we need everyone to become a fully functional social system.

There are different people, who will have different likings, different energy levels, different tendencies and may be different faiths.

Should we respect everyone's faith.
Absolutely!

Should any reason deter us to value other's faith?
No!

Is it justified to eradicate everyone who doesn't have the same faith as one's?
No!

Is it ever justified to be so indulged in one's faith that everything else feels negative and worthy of eradication?
No!

Is it ever justified to force anyone to change their faith to appease one's?
No!

Faith is the anchor around which lives hold on. Shaking that or taking that away from someone may cause a lot of unrest. Not just this, it my make the other person feel disrespected to the core.

Faith come from within and should always be at free will.

Staying respectful and tolerant of the differences between people is very important to work in harmony and to survive.

Anyone who wants to de-value a life for a piece of land, money, power, converting other's faith and especially if uses force to obtain any of the aforesaid, is definitely not going to bring them close to heaven.

Giving anyone, miseries can never result in a reward be it during or after life.

We are humans and are evolved. We should behave like human and use emotions that separates humans with rest of the animal kingdom.

It is sad to see that some human acts are such, that they can be taught kindness by the most ruthless animals.

Let the variations thrive, if they become scarce, help them grow back. Every variation has a value. One should follow one's heart but forcing others to follow the same one's heart is wrong. Everyone should have the freedom to follow their hearts.

When anyone tries to forcefully change other's journey, one only adds additional load to one's bag of karma to dissolve eventually which simply means that heaven just got pushed farther.

If one wants to bring heaven closer, the best way is to create one around one where everyone can live happily and safely!

Heartfelt condolences to all those who have lost their loved ones because some other person could not see them being different or because they had something that someone wanted to have at any cost.

May the innocent souls rest in peace!

History teaches a lot. Future should be better not worse than the past.

May the light fall upon those who caused the miseries so they can see in the light, how dark such acts are!

Such acts can certainly never be heavenly!

Photograph by: Dr. Jaya Sonkar MD MPH

Photograph by: Dr. Jaya Sonkar MD MPH

4. ONLY PRESENT IS REAL

Let's say, if real can be described as what we can touch, we can touch what is there at this time.

Anything that is past is untouchable and it only exists in memory (either human memory, or electronic memory or lost in time).

Anything that is the future only exists in imagination until it becomes present when it becomes a reality.

The present is precious because that is the only real thing that we have and it will become a memory in just one second.

Every second, another present becomes past.

While past, present and future can be interconnected, the action phase is only in the present.

If we spend time thinking about the past or the future, we are wasting a way the only real thing that we have and which will not wait for us as it is turning into past every second by second.

That means this present that we have is precious and unique and will never return to us. So if we want to make a difference, we need to act in present and live this present and absorb this present and that can turn past into fond memories and that can turn future into a beautiful present.

The same applies to the people and things.

Whoever was in the past is no longer real unless that same person is in the present.

Whoever is in the present may no longer be there in the next moment.

Whoever is expected in the future is not real until comes in the present.

Same applies for things.

Can we go back in the past and relive it. Can we control the forces of nature in the future?

The only one thing that we have in our hands is what we have in the present.

The views, the sounds, the people, the things, and ourselves in present.

These are our companions in the present.

And present should be our focus.

If there was a delete button in our mind and let's say that memory of the past is erased, then anything that gave us any sort of feeling would not affect us in any which way. It would neither have the potential to make us happy nor sad.

It would just become non existent.

That means what we make of our past is the play of our memory.

The memory is needed to function fully in the present.

If we can control the memory and choose to erase anything that was not pleasant, we can stay very pleasant at all the times.

If we program our memories with the data that we would like to see, it can now make us the happiest ever.

Basically, it's our hard drive and we should only keep the life movies that gave us rich learning experiences and make us feel accomplished and pleasant.

Delete the rest of the unwanted memories into the archive of our minds. It's always beneficial to have them archived so they are available if needed in the future but that way it won't take too much space in the present.

And our present will be wholly available to experience and perform and make new memories which can be kept in the main folder of our brain or archive.

Present is where we can make a difference and present is the only time when we can collect more happy past and create more happy future.

Focus on the present time and present company and present activity is the most productive and fruitful way of living.

And this life which is present, who knows when it will become past and it sure will happen.

The choice is ours. Do we want to waste it or live it?

Let's live each moment as if it is the only opportunity to live this moment in the eternal time, because... that is actually true!

Photograph by: Dr. Jaya Sonkar MD MPH

5. THE GRANDEUR – WHAT DOES IT TELL US?

When something is grand, it doesn't need to demonstrate its grandeur anymore. It just has it — and it doesn't care about having it.

Because it is simply grand, and there is nothing to prove, no one to impress. It just stands tall in its own glory.

Be it the Empire State Building, the Eiffel Tower, or any grand structure. Be it an ocean, a canyon, a mountain, or the sky. And be it any accomplished person.

There are no words needed and no actions done. They are just there.

Look at a tall waterfall — Niagara, Yosemite, or any other. It keeps on running the show as long as it can. As long as it has life, it will show the power of water falling from a height.

It will continually create the thundering sound. It doesn't care about the time of day, the presence or absence of an audience, or anything else.

It just keeps on going. It doesn't care if it is being compared with any other waterfall or any other grand structure.

It just does what it is supposed to — and it does it really well, unaffected.

Isn't it a miracle to be alive?
Life itself is grand, and every life should treat itself with the grand respect it deserves.

Without caring to impress anyone. Without concern for praise or criticism.

A life should just do its job — which is to LIVE, fully and unstoppably, until it stops. Unaffected by anything or anyone.

And that's the Empire State of Mind.

Photograph by: Dr. Jaya Sonkar MD MPH

6. MULTI RELIGIONISM

What is better?
Knowing one language
Being Bilingual
Or
Being Multilingual

What is better?
Having one treatment modality?
Having two treatment modalities?
Or
Having multiple treatment modalities?

What is better?
Having access to one country?
Having access to two countries?
Or
Having access to multiple countries?

What is better?
Having one person on the earth?
Having two persons on the earth?
Or
Having multiple persons on the earth?

Can we say that:

Everything has pros and cons.
Everything has strengths and flaws.
What is good for one can be bad for the other?
What is easy for one can be difficult for the other?
What is good to follow for one can be hard to follow
for another?
What is easy to have faith in for one can be difficult
for another?
Can we say that everything can have two sides?

Then,
Can we say that all religions can have something
good and something not so good?

Then,
Can we say that following many religions and grasping the pros from all is better than following just one or two?

In such a scenario, can we say that orthodoxy to one can never be good?

Can we agree that harming someone physically or mentally is not good?

Can we agree that Non-Violence is the most productive way to live and build a society globally?

Can we agree that if we imbibe the goodness and healthy habits and ethics from all religions and not condemn any, it will be beneficial for one and all?

Can we say that having absolute freedom for anyone to adopt any faith or many faiths would be good?

Can we say that if we follow Humanism, and be true humans and use our emotions and follow all the good preaching from all religions and follow the religion of medicine to stay and keep everyone healthy, it would be good?

Can we agree that following the simple rules as mentioned below may bring peace and harmony:

- Do no harm to anyone
- Try to make it easy for others without making it hard for self
- Live and let live
- Do not interfere with anyone's free will
- Let everyone follow their chosen faith or faiths and adapt to their chosen lifestyle
- Do not force any clothing or dressing style on anyone, male or female
- People should be able to wear what they want. Anything or everything

Regardless of faith, women should have equal rights as men in all religions and should have the freedom to wear, walk, and behave freely regardless of the religion.

The most advanced culture has men who protect their women's free will and men who have self-control instead of the power to control their women.

Can we say that what we expect from others should first be expected from ourselves?

Monogamy is good for raising families.
However, if anyone believes in polygamy, then can we agree that that someone should allow polygamy to that someone's partner too? And if that someone can't allow that, then that someone should not do it either.

People should be able to eat what they want and honor others' choices too.

People should adapt healthy habits from all faiths.

Mindfulness, physical exercises, fresh fruits and vegetables, and plant-based diets and lean white meats are better than sugars, carbohydrates, red meat, and shellfish.

Can we follow evidence-based modern medical science as a religion instead of following eminence-based rules when it comes to health and lifestyle?

Can we say that we don't need leaders in any religion?

Can we say we can lead our own faith in whichever way we want?

And if we agree, can we answer as mentioned below when asked what's our religion?

We are Humans and follow Humanism, and Humanism is multireligionism that adapts the best from all faiths, respects all faiths, and respectfully avoids any harmful practices from any faith.

And if you agree that this could be beneficial in any way, can I ask for your support to please share this thought forward in an attempt to make the world more beautiful, more peaceful, and more livable?

Photograph by: Dr. Jaya Sonkar MD MPH

Poems

Dr. Jaya Sonkar MD MPH

मेरे साथी मेरे हमसफ़र

मेरे साथी मेरे हमसफ़र
बड़ी लंबी सी है ये डगर

करने हैं मुझे काम कई मगर
लगता है कभी थोड़ा सा डर

वक़्त थोड़ा ठहर जाए अगर
देख लूं सलोनी शाम पल भर

ताप लूं सुनहरी धूप दम भर
समां लूं थोड़ा सा आसमान अंदर

मेरे साथी मेरे हमसफ़र
बड़ा अनोखा रहा है ये सफ़र

कुछ ढूंढ रही मेरी नज़र
कुछ सोचता है मन चारों पहर

क्या खोया क्या पाया, क्या हुआ असर
क्या लाएगी कल फिर नई सेहर

मेरे साथी मेरे हमसफ़र
जाग उठी है एक नई लहर

ढल रहा है सूरज, तब भी पर
एक नई सुबह का है इंतज़ार

क्या भीगे हुए पंछियों के पर
ले जा पाएंगे उन्हें समंदर पार

मेरे साथी मेरे हमसफ़र
बड़ा लंबा है ये सफ़र

क्या इसके अंत होने पर
होंगे हम साथ हर पहर

क्या अंत के बाद भी
ढूंढ लोगे मेरी खोई डगर

मेरे साथी मेरे हमसफ़र
मेरे साथी मेरे हमसफ़र

English Translation

MY FRIEND, MY COMPAN-ION

My friend, my companion
It's a very long road

I have many things to do
But sometimes I get scared

I wish the time could pause
So I could observe the beautiful evening

Get some warmth from the afternoon sun
And absorb a bit of sky within

My friend my companion
It has been a unique journey

There is something that my eyes are looking for
There is something that my mind is searching for

What's lost, what is gained and what was the effect

My friend my companion
A new wave is rising within

The sun is setting
And I am waiting for a new morning

Would the birds with wet wings
Be able to cross the oceans

My friend my companion
This is a very long road

Would you be there
When it comes to an end

Would you be able to find me
Even after all ends

My friend my companion
My friend my companion!

Dr. Jaya Sonkar MD MPH

सब सही है, सब सही!

एक नहीं तो और सही
और नहीं तो और सही
मीत नहीं तो गैर सही
प्रीत नहीं तो बैर सही

तीर नहीं तो कमान सही
घर नहीं तो मकान सही
राज नहीं तो ताज सही
पहचान के मोहताज नहीं

सुर नहीं तो ताल सही
गीत नहीं तो साज़ सही

गूंजते से सन्नाटे में
धड़कन की आवाज़ सही

ऊँच नहीं तो नीच सही
वृक्ष नहीं तो बीज सही
जल नहीं तो रेत सही
दावत नहीं तो भेंट सही

दिन नहीं तो रात सही
सूरज नहीं तो चाँद सही
जीत नहीं तो मात सही
बोल न हो पर बात सही

सौ नहीं तो शून्य सही
शून्य से ही आए सभी
मूल नहीं तो परछाई सही
परछाई से ही मुलाक़ात सही

सब सही है, सब सही
कुछ भी बेमतलब नहीं
हर चीज़ का गहरा अर्थ है
अर्थ भी सही, अनर्थ भी सही

जीवन का पूरा सार यही
सब सही है, सब सही!

English Translation

EVERYTHING IS RIGHT , EVERYTHING IS RIGHT

If not one, there is another
If not another, there is still an other
If not known, strangers are fine
If not love, enmity is fine

If there isn't an arrow, a bow is just fine
If there is not a home, a building is just fine
If there is no empire, a throne is just fine
Its ok if there is no fame, we aren't defined by any
name

If there are no notes, the beats are just fine
If there is no song, the melody is just fine
In the echoing silence, the sound of the heartbeat is
just fine

If not the highs, the lows are just fine
If there isn't a tree, the seed is just fine
If there is no water, the sand is just fine
If there is no fiesta, a gift is just fine

If it isn't a day, the night is just fine
If the sun isn't shining, fine is the moonshine
If there isn't a win, a loss is just fine
If there is no victory, defeat is just fine
If there are no words, the silent meaning is just
fine

If there isn't a hundred, a zero is just fine
After all, every thing emerged from a vacuum
If the body isn't there, the shadow is just fine
The shadow is enough for the tryst with the soul

Everything is fine, everything is fine
There is nothing that is without a purpose
Everything has a deep meaning
The good is fine and the bad is just fine

This is the gist of life
Everything is Right, Everything is fine

Photograph by: Dr. Jaya Sonkar MD MPH

BEAUTY IS IN THE EYES OF THE BEHOLDER

Beauty is in the eyes of the beholder
Filth is in the eyes of the perpetrator

Dreams are in the mind of an achiever
Fear is in the mind of a failure

Faith is in the heart of a believer
Doubt is in the heart of a traitor

Wealth is in the richness of actions
Penury is in the poverty of forbearance

Victory is in the bravery
Defeat is in the cowardice

Stability is in the calm
Turmoil is in the chaos

Love is in the selflessness
Hatred is in the selfishness

Grace is in the eyes of the beholder
Beauty is in the eyes of the beholder

Photograph by: Dr. Jaya Sonkar MD MPH

I FOUND MYSELF

I saw the mirror many times
But today, I saw myself
I saw my eyes
I saw my tears
I saw my smiles
I saw my fears
I saw my cries
I saw my cheers

I saw the mirror many times
But today, I felt myself
I felt the kind
I felt the unkind

I felt the easy
I felt the tough
I felt the soft
I felt the rough
I felt the joy
I felt the sorrow
I felt the cotton
I felt the rock
I felt the pleasant
I felt the anger

I saw the mirror many times
But today, I met with myself

Who am I?

I am not just my eyes
I am not just my ears
I am not just my lips
I am not just my hair
I am not just my skin
I have a deeper inside
I am not just a body
I have a beautiful mind
I am not perfect
I have my flaws
I have my moments
Of fire and ice

I have the strength
I have the weakness

I saw the mirror many times
But today, I found myself
I had my nightmares
I had my dreams
I had my failures
I had my success
I had my losses
I had my wins
I lost some on the way
I found some on the way
But most importantly
I saw a new me
I found me on the way
Metamorphosized
Determined
To continue to grow
Continue to evolve

I saw the mirror many times,
But today, I found growth
I found realization
That growth comes with all

Positives or negatives
Thicks or Thins

Growth comes with
Anything and everything

I saw the mirror many times
But today, I thanked it
For showing the me
Beyond me
Because
I found myself

Photograph by: Dr. Jaya Sonkar MD MPH

Dr. Jaya Sonkar MD MPH

LOVE IS ENDLESS!

For the parents who lost their children
For the children who lost their parents
For the siblings who lost their siblings
For the spouses who lost their spouses
For the friends who lost their friends
For anyone who lost anyone

The loss is always there
The grief is always there
The memories are always there
So is the love...
The love is always there
The love is both sided

It travels through the boundaries
Of Life and Death

It's like the light that's received from the stars
millions of miles away
Sometimes it's visible
Sometimes we need special lens
And sometimes we just need
An imagintion and perception

Sooner or later, it always happens
We learn to perceive
We learn to believe
We learn to cope
We learn to hope
We learn to live
We learn to give
We learn what's there
We learn what's here
We learn about death
We learn about faith

After all, aren't we alive
When we are asleep
Aren't we alive

When a part of the body is not
Aren't we receptive

When senses are shut
Aren't we awakened
To start a new day

Could it be
That life is a chapter
And the book is endless
Could it be
That after the end
A new chapter begins
Could it be
That the end is only
A beginning of new beginnings

For the parents who lost their children
For the children who lost their parents
For the siblings who lost their siblings
For the spouses who lost their spouses
For the friends who lost their friends
For anyone who lost anyone

We can only do what we can
While we are limited with our bodily presence
But our minds can do
What is unlimited
We can reach places
We can believe the endless
We can have faith in the impossible

We can love selflessly and endlessly
Selfless love is the key to the eternal calm

We can selflessly shower
The love and blessings
On those who ever were
On those who will not be
On those who are around
On those who we surround!

Because,
Love is Selfless
Love is Endless
With lots of deep thoughts

Photograph by: Dr. Jaya Sonkar MD MPH

NOTHING TO LOSE

Nothing to lose!

There is nothing to lose.

It's true that
There is wealth to lose

It's true that
There is health to lose

It's true that
There is love to lose

It's true that
There is dove to lose
But no one asked
To not maintain this

No one asked to
Abandon these

If we see the process
Of making a sandcastle
Hard work, time, and effort to build
Were phasic joys that give an experience
That effort also
Led to an attachment

But can the sandcastle
Be there forever?
It will mingle with the rest
Sooner or later

What's there today
Won't be tomorrow
But what's there today
May take a new shape
And evolve tomorrow

Where were we 100 years ago?
Where will we be 100 years later?

We don't know
But clearly, its a journey
From somewhere unknown
To somewhere unknown
And whatever we know
Will merge into that unknown
While the present will be lost The past will be known
And the future will be gained

The wind will blow
From one place to another
The water will flow
From one place to another
The planets will revolve
Around one sun or another
The vacuum will be there
In the entire space
It's said
Energy is never lost
It only changes from
One form to another
And so will we...

What we can do is
Use the energy
In whichever form it is
In the best possible way

And create
A best possible experience!

While there seems to be
A lot to lose
There actually is
Nothing to lose!!!

Photograph by: Dr. Jaya Sonkar MD MPH

Dr. Jaya Sonkar MD MPH

THE END

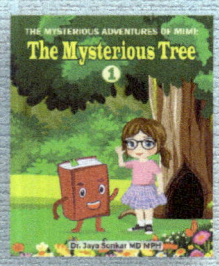

THE MYSTERIOUS ADVENTURES OF MIMI:
The Mysterious Tree ①

Dr. Jaya Sonkar MD MPH

THE MYSTERIOUS ADVENTURES OF MIMI:
THE MYSTERIOUS GLASSES ②

Dr. Jaya Sonkar MD MPH

THE MYSTERIOUS ADVENTURES OF MIMI:
THE MYSTERIOUS BACKPACK ③

Dr. Jaya Sonkar MD MPH

THE MYSTERIOUS ADVENTURES OF MIMI:
THE MAGICAL MIRROR ④

Dr. Jaya Sonkar MD MPH

THE MYSTERIOUS ADVENTURES OF MIMI:
MIMI AND THE MYSTERY OF THE SPARKLY DUST ⑤

Dr. Jaya Sonkar MD MPH

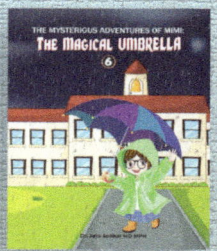

THE MYSTERIOUS ADVENTURES OF MIMI:
THE MAGICAL UMBRELLA ⑥

Dr. Jaya Sonkar MD MPH

THE MYSTERIOUS ADVENTURES OF MIMI:
THE MAGIC TRASH CAN ⑦

Dr. Jaya Sonkar MD MPH

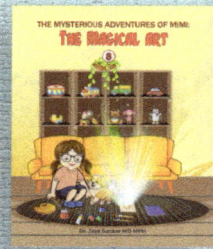

THE MYSTERIOUS ADVENTURES OF MIMI:
THE MAGICAL ART ⑧

Dr. Jaya Sonkar MD MPH

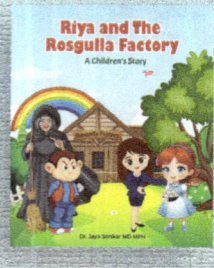

Riya and The Rosgulla Factory
A Children's Story

Dr. Jaya Sonkar MD MPH

Ridiculously Simplified Rheumatology
The Story Of Mr. Gout!
VOL ①
Dr. Jaya Sonkar
MD, MPH

THE MYSTERIOUS ADVENTURES OF MIMI:
Mimi and the Copycat ⑨

Dr. Jaya Sonkar MD MPH

THE MYSTERIOUS ADVENTURES OF MIMI:
MIMI AND THE DR. MIMI SUPERHERO ⑩

Dr. Jaya Sonkar MD MPH

JEEVAN GYAN
Life Lessons

Dr. Jaya Sonkar MD MPH

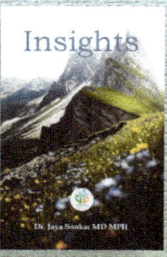

Insights

Dr. Jaya Sonkar MD MPH

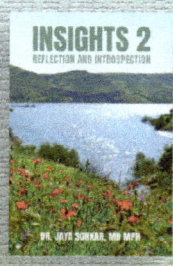

INSIGHTS 2
REFLECTION AND INTROSPECTION

Dr. Jaya Sonkar, MD MPH

Insights 3
A Journey Beyond Boundaries

Dr. Jaya Sonkar, MD MPH

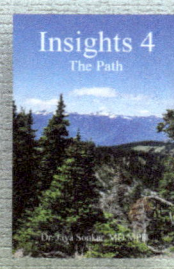

Insights 4
The Path

Dr. Jaya Sonkar, MD MPH